Non-negotiables

Non-negotiables

A guide to school management

Fake Headteacher

3

Email

headteachernewsletter@outlook.com

Web

www.headteacher-newsletter.com

Twitter & Facebook

@fakeheadteacher

Disclaimer

Some of this book is fictitious.

It depends where you work as to how much.

If I have described how your Head manages your school, you have my sympathy. The similarities are completely coincidental, and I accept no responsibility for their numpty ways.

Contents

Foreword

When Fake Headteacher approached me to write a foreword for his new book, I jumped at the chance.

I have had the pleasure of working with Fake Headteacher for many years, before letting him go due to staff restructuring within the academy.

We spotted his talent very early on during the interview process.

He made no attempt to bond with the staff during lunch and was very happy to criticise teachers as he carried out a learning walk with us. He was able to pick up scores of problems in each class and explained how his micro-managing of staff would eradicate the problems within weeks.

His ability to get the very best from his staff, ensuring they worked late into the evening and weekends, was to be admired.

He batted away any unrest with arrogance and determination, introducing capability procedures without hesitation.

He knows how to increase exam results at any cost and cares very little for staff and pupil wellbeing.

We were extremely pleased with his style of management and despite having to send our human resources officer in most weeks to deal with teacher union complaints - he was one of our most highly regarded Headteachers within the academy.

And now, you too can learn how to become as effective as Fake Headteacher. This book is an essential read for anyone wanting to improve their school and move quickly up the leadership ladder.

Mr Dick

Requires Improvement MAT Director

11

Introduction

It gives me great pleasure to be able to share my leadership experiences with you in this inspiring new book.

Whether you are a teacher looking to become a Head one day, or you are already a Head looking for new ideas, or even interested in overseeing a cluster of schools in your area, this book is for you.

I was very fortunate that I only had to work in one school before I was snapped up for my first Headship role. Although my classroom experience was limited, I had what it took to become the leader I am today.

A colleague of mine once said, 'Great football managers weren't necessarily great players.' I couldn't agree more. It's not always necessary to have taught for very long or indeed, to have been very good at it.

I have read lots of books on how to become a good leader and my cold, heartless style has certainly helped me become the Head others are aspiring to become.

'Non-negotiables – a guide to school management', will support you completely in managing your school. Dip in and out of it as you please.

Remember, it's lonely at the top. Keep it that way.

Fake Headteacher

Assemblies

Your first assembly at a school is very important. Everyone will be judging you. You must make the right impression.

You must win over pupils with something fun. They will normally be well behaved for your first assembly because they'll be a little anxious. Make sure teachers know how good you are.

Make sure your first assembly is inspiring and motivational. Staff will gossip about the assembly at break time. This will be your first test. Don't fall at the first hurdle. It must be an all-singing and all-dancing assembly.

Once your first assembly is out of the way, ask staff to attend all of your future assemblies. It makes it easier to manage the pupils when staff are there. Why should *you* have to struggle? You're the Headteacher.

You must only take one assembly a week. Teachers will have to sort the rest out themselves.

Always turn up slightly late for assemblies so teachers must deal with the behaviour. It's a real nuisance having to sort this out when you are at the front. You can be the good cop in this situation. Turn up and smile.

If assemblies run over, do not allow extra break time. You must think ahead for SATs. Every minute of learning counts.

Make sure you ask a member of staff to organise your assemblies. For example, get them to ask pupils to sort out the songs, chairs and the laptop. Done right, you should be able to walk in last minute and it will be all done for you.

You must take a register of staff who are late or don't turn up at all for your assemblies. Some will try to get away with it. They will fail.

After a few weeks, ask the deputy or a keen assistant Head to take your assemblies on occasion. Have a rest.

You should seriously think about organising a celebration assembly too on a Friday but some weeks, try to arrange long meetings so you don't have to do them. That's what your deputy is for.

You must have an attendance cup. Ofsted are hot on attendance so make sure you put pressure on the pupils.

Every week make sure you tell the school which classes are underperforming and which classes are excelling.

Consider telling each class the percentage of pupils who made it to school over the week. Round the percentages to two decimal places to make it more interesting. For example: 93.45%.

Give out awards to classes and individuals to encourage pupils to be punctual and to stay healthy. Name and shame if you need to.

Some Heads reward pupils with book vouchers and iPads for 100% attendance each term.

There will be some pupils who can't help having time off and may be bullied because they consistently let the class down. You must be strong and ignore this. Your attendance percentages mean more to you.

One way to win over parents is to ask staff to write out eight, star-of-the-week certificates for each class. Always call it the Headteacher's award ceremony. Pupils will go home and say what an amazing Head you are.

Take photos of you and the children and put it in the newsletter - all to boost your reputation. Put up a Headteacher's award display in the front entrance too, to show visitors how amazing you are.

If you can't be bothered dismissing pupils at the end of the assembly, ask staff to take their own classes out when they are ready.

This saves you the hassle of dealing with behaviour and you can chat to some pupils at the front. If the children are noisy, tell staff off in the next staff meeting. Remind staff that pupils must leave the hall silently. Make it their problem, not yours.

Make sure staff write, rehearse and perform class assemblies to parents every half term. It's a public relations thing. Tell staff it's low key but criticise them if the assemblies are not good enough. They will soon be planning all-singing and all-dancing ones.

If pupils are naughty in assembly, make sure they miss their playtimes but get the teachers to supervise them. You will have coffee to drink before your next meeting.

Ideally, try to keep up to date with current affairs so you can feed them into your assembly.

If possible, follow the whole school weekly theme but it's often easier to sing a couple of songs and remind them about school uniform etc. It's quicker and takes less preparation.

A keen assistant Head can always do a more serious one in the week. You must find time to focus on other things.

On occasion, you may feel very tired because you were out the night before. Don't let the staff see your weakness as you struggle to keep control of the assembly.

Instead, tell staff they don't need to be in. They will be ecstatic and walk out smiling. They will love you for it. Then put YouTube on, sing some pop songs and talk about current affairs. Easy.

Consider being very moody in one assembly once a month. Really moody. Get cross. Raise your voice a little. It's just an act. Pick anything to moan about. Make it up if you must. It's a good strategy. It reminds the pupils who is the boss.

It sends a little reminder to the staff too that you have what it takes to kick butt.

Perhaps in the same moody assembly, ban football at break times for a week. There doesn't need to be a reason. Just do it. It's a quick, non-confrontational way of showing the pupils you're in charge. In your next assembly, you can reinstate it, saying how proud you are of the children because of their improved behaviour. It's a power thing. It works a treat.

If parents attend an assembly, make sure you smile, make jokes, and come across as an entirely charming and caring Headteacher that can't do any wrong. Parents will think you're amazing and worship the ground you walk on. You will look great compared to the tired and stressed teachers sitting on the side. Be aware of eye-rolling from teachers. Make sure you pick up on this later.

If a parent brings in a noisy toddler during an assembly, ask a teacher to deal with it. Ideally, ask them to tell the parent to leave.

Under no circumstances should *you* ask the parent to leave. It will make you look mean and it will be all over social media within the hour. Alternatively, just smile through the agonising noise as pupils are trying to read out their work.

Always deliver a small speech after a class assembly to parents. Obviously praise the class and say things like, 'Let's give them another round of applause!' Standard. But use this time to remind parents of all the great things the school is doing and how much progress the children are making.

You must promote your school and your reputation at all costs. Do this even if the assembly has overrun. Try to use words such as creative curriculum, standards, progress, excellence, opportunities, outstanding. Quote things from recent Ofsted and HMI reports that sound good.

If possible, invite local church leaders in to take assemblies. Make sure it's on your assembly day though. Tell staff they must stay in. *You* don't need to stay. Delegate.

When Ofsted arrive, carry out an assembly but insist teachers and teaching assistants attend. Place some flowers on the piano, light a few candles and choose some nice songs to sing. Start the intervention group for the 'tricky' children that morning (run by a TA) – keep them away from Ofsted.

Ask children to join in a prayer. Invite your more able Year 6s up to read some thought-provoking poems. Dig out that snazzy PowerPoint you found on Twinkl. Mention Christianity at least once and probably the words 'collective worship'. In addition, I would try to link something to British values. When they leave the school, return to whatever you did before. Tick that box.

Think about standing behind a small podium for that extra authoritative presence. Or, have a tall stool at the front to sit on. Demand that attention. To look very cool, wear a radio mic. Ask one of the teachers to take a photograph of you, mid-assembly, with your hands in the air with a great PowerPoint slide in the background.

Use this photo for all your social media profile images. It'll look great.

Book Scrutiny

For books to look their best, repeat the phrase 'It's all about the books' at least once a week. Mention it as much as you can. I can't emphasise this enough. You will thank me. You simply can't trust staff to teach well so make the books look great to hide any poor teaching. It's also a control thing. You need to micro-manage staff.

Make sure teachers mark pupil premium books first. They should mark these books excessively. Ideally, there should be double the amount of written feedback in these books.

Think about asking staff to colour code pupil premium books so they can be quickly found after the lesson.

Equally, any pupils that have been identified as exceeding must have a similar amount of written feedback but only once the pupil premium books have been looked at first.

You must not trust teachers to share the learning objective properly in lessons. So, make sure learning objectives are typed up and stuck on each page. They must include a success criterion (at least 5 bullet points) so even if the lesson is bad, Ofsted can still see what learning was meant to occur.

The slips make it easier for any observer of books to see what the pupils were learning on that day (in case they can't work it out for themselves). It has nothing to do with the pupils' learning; *they* know what they did. The slips generate a lot of work for staff but that's ok.

Make sure you police the type of learning objectives that are being used. They must not be too wishy-washy and be at least 20 words long. You must check the quality of learning objectives and quickly discipline staff if needed.

Learning objectives must be typed up and printed in the way you like them.

Some learning objective slips might have more words on than pupils write in the lesson, but this is fine. It's better to have the teacher prove competence in their subject. This trumps any concerns about workload issues involved in creating the slips.

Staff will hate doing them. They will probably ask if the pupils can write the learning objective instead. Refuse. It's all about consistency. Every book must look the same.

Ofsted don't really care how the learning objective is shared but they will ask the children what they are learning. Teach pupils how to regurgitate the learning objective from the slip. Consider rehearsing this process every day.

Make sure the correct font and font size is used on the learning objective slip. Any deviation from this must be dealt with swiftly.

To make the perfect learning objective slip, leave space for some blank traffic lights or circles for children to colour in - to show how they feel about their learning. It's a waste of time really and teachers don't look at them, but it looks good. Everything is about appearance.

Why not ask staff to add a tick box on the same slip where the teacher can say whether the pupil did the work independently or not.

All lessons need one of the learning objective slips in books. Remember, it's for observers of books, not for the pupils. They look great.

The long date must be written in all books by the pupil. It must be underlined 2mm underneath the text. This must be part of the book scrutiny. It makes all the difference to the look you are trying to create for observers.

The short date is allowed in maths books but the same 2mm underline rule must apply.

Ensure deep marking occurs at least three times a week. A deep mark is where the teacher must provide evidence that they have read the work and know how to improve it. A deep mark ensures that all spelling and grammar is picked up and three next steps must be written out.

Again, this proves to you and to Ofsted that the teacher can do their job. Without next steps, how does anyone know the teacher has given feedback?

To prove the pupil has made progress after the teacher has written the next steps, make the pupils respond in a different colour. It makes it so obvious that the pupil has responded to the teacher's feedback and progress has occurred. Easy.

Also, other schools are doing it so it must work. I've not personally researched it. But you don't want to get left behind.

Highlighter pens are fantastic. Teachers should highlight words in one colour to show that it's good. Do not accept teachers ticking words they like (especially double ticking for very good bits).

Teachers must also highlight things in another colour to show what the pupil must improve. I insist you ask teachers to use highlighters. It smacks Ofsted in the face when they look at books. It's all about the books. Play the game.

Consider asking teachers to highlight the learning objective too, to inform the pupil if they understood the lesson. This must be done for every pupil of course.

On top of this, it's worth using two stars and a wish at least once a week. It's another tool with which staff can prove feedback has occurred.

Some schools have ditched some of these old favourites for verbal feedback only. Do not do this yet. You simply can't afford for Ofsted not to see feedback being given. It's your reputation on the line. Staff will have to work doubly hard, but it will pay dividends when you get the good judgement.

Make sure the teacher checks every day that a pupil has responded in purple pen to any feedback given by the teacher.

Consider dropping reading time to ensure this always happens. Give it a fancy name like 'Purple Pen Feedback Fun'.

Teachers should tell children in class to silently respond to the written feedback. Then get teachers to check pupils' responses to their feedback before adding any further comments in the book. Purple pen use also demonstrates clearly that pupils can edit their work. Excellent evidence.

I would suggest the following coloured pens are used for your marking policy:

Black: Teacher feedback
Blue: Teaching assistant feedback
Orange: Peer feedback
Purple: Pupil responding to feedback
Green highlighter: Teacher feedback (praise)
Pink highlighter: Teacher feedback (even better if)

Ban the use of written praise in books by staff. Pupils might like it and it might inspire them to work harder, but it will not help them learn.

Ofsted will want to see next steps. Don't let staff waste time writing praise.

Concentrate on what the pupil must do to improve. It's never good enough as far as I am concerned. As for stickers to motivate, forget it.

Staff must follow the correct handwriting style that the pupils use. Every letter should be checked when you carry out a book scrutiny. It takes time to check but all descenders and ascenders must be formed correctly by staff.

All letters that should join, must be joined. Letters 'f, k, x and z' must be formed correctly according to the school style. To ensure this is done, name and shame teachers in staff meetings if you feel you need to. It's all about the books.

Under no circumstances should pupils go back and use up blank pages. It completely ruins the golden thread of learning. What would Ofsted say when they see some work that has no place in the middle of a unit of work on story writing. This is unacceptable.

Insist staff stick any blank pages together or write an apology note on the page, explaining what happened. Staff must hold pupils accountable for any pages missed.

Consider using break times to discipline pupils if they have blank pages in their books. They'll soon learn about the golden thread of learning. Blank pages just look bad. Work written on the wrong page looks even worse. It's all about the books.

Reception children must join their letters. It's a data thing. The more children who join letters, the easier it becomes to say they are meeting expectations later. You must make sure they do it.

Key Stage 1 teachers must write long next step comments in books too. The pupils can't read them, but it just looks good and shows evidence of feedback given.

Under no circumstances should pupils use pen until they can meet the high handwriting standards. Pupils must consistently write in their absolute best handwriting. All the time.

To be considered for a pen licence, make pupils show you at least fifty pieces of work which are written immaculately. For some pupils, this will never be achievable but don't worry about that.

You will get a larger majority of pupils who will be using pen by Year 6 and their presentation will be amazing. Everything will look the same, but the books will look great. It's all about the books.

To ensure spelling is correct, always ask staff to give pupils a spelling mat to use - especially common exception words and relevant spelling lists for each year group. It means you can say they spelt the words independently in moderation meetings.

It also gives the impression that spelling in school is being taught exceptionally well. It looks good because most schools struggle with spelling standards.

Pupils must explain their thinking in maths every single day. Teachers should write comments such as, 'Why?', 'How do you know?' and 'Prove it' at least three times a week.

Don't worry too much whether the calculations are correct. No one cares about that anymore. Explain, reason, prove it. That's it. Pupils should be expected to write at least ten sentences in maths every lesson. It has taken over. No need for numbers and calculations. It is what it is. Things have changed.

Consider introducing a long marking code full of symbols for staff and pupils to learn. I would recommend about eighteen symbols. These can be used in addition to all the other forms of written feedback. Squiggles, circles, triangles, ladders and hearts work particularly well.

Ensure these are used regularly to prove a whole school approach is being adhered to. Under no circumstances should you allow staff to use their own codes.

Think about using a tally system to count how many times each week the codes are being used. Some staff will refuse to use them, or not use them enough so be aware. Quickly deal with this.

You must also enforce a verbal feedback policy. Staff *must* talk to the pupils about how to improve their work. To prove this has occurred, teachers must write the letters VF in pupils' books. Aim for about four each lesson. To make it more effective, ask teachers to annotate what the verbal feedback was, and what the pupil did in response. Perfect.

Any verbal feedback given must be evidenced otherwise how will you know that the teacher has spoken to the pupil? I know progress will be seen over time if the teacher has consistently given verbal feedback, but it must be evidenced somehow to let Ofsted know it has occurred.

Verbal feedback stampers are popular. You can buy them online quite cheaply nowadays. Just ensure teachers write a summary of what was said next to the stamp.

Peer feedback is quite the fashion at the moment so ensure staff give opportunities for pupils to give written feedback to their peers. Play the game. Staff must insist pupils do it. I suggest at least two times a week to be safe.

Some pupils will complain because they don't want their 'talk buddy' writing messily in their book. Tough.

Pupils must write feedback comments on scrap paper first so the teacher can mark it for spelling before the pupil copies it into their friend's book. It's all about the books.

Ensure staff take photos of the pupils working at least once a week. These photos can be uploaded onto the website and blog. But more importantly, they can be printed and stuck into books to show Ofsted how happy the pupils are when they are working. It takes staff time to complete but it makes the books look great.

You can also use the photos to gauge what is going on in lessons. Win-win. Make sure all photos are the correct size in all books. I suggest 8cm x 4cm. Consistency must be your priority.

All staff must identify at least four pupils after every lesson to have a 'same day intervention'. It doesn't matter if they don't need one, but it looks good. Make sure staff annotate the book to explain that the pupils have been out for a 'same day intervention' and to annotate how it went. It looks great for Ofsted. It's quite the craze.

Many experienced teachers will resist your book scrutiny non-negotiables. They will want to use their own experience and style of feedback to make sure pupils make good progress. You must not allow staff to start doing their own thing.

Having non-negotiables for books ensures you can stamp your authority and use it to come down on staff if you need to. It's better to micro-manage staff so you can control everyone. You will be asked by observers what you are doing to improve the school. You can show them your book non-negotiables list. Easy.

So, you have your non-negotiables. You must now ensure you carry out book scrutiny checks at least fortnightly. Bullet point everything mentioned in this guide and use it to grade teachers against it. Some Heads like to see evidence for each bullet point every week. Staff must pass everything on the list to avoid being put on a support plan (or even capabilities).

Books in each year group must look identical and help prove to Ofsted that staff are following your policy. You must come down hard on any members of staff not following your non-negotiables.

It is advisable to have secret book scrutinies. Do them once staff have gone home. Have a wander around the school and pick up random books to check. If you notice anything you are concerned about, ask for books from all the staff the very next morning.

Even better still, don't *ask* for the books. Collect them personally. This way, you stop teachers adding in last minute additions to satisfy your non-negotiables. They will do this. I promise.

If you need to, do an unannounced learning walk to target those teachers whose books didn't meet your standards. You can easily pick up on the books in the lesson and then discipline the teacher later.

Consider naming and shaming year groups in staff meetings if they are not keeping up with your demands. It must always be about the books. Always. Progress in books must be secondary to everything else on the non-negotiables list. I know this sounds strange but it's true. The books must look good.

Progress is also harder to gauge quickly. You would have to *read* the work. But it's easier to have lots of things on a list that are measurable and easily identifiable. For example: learning objective slips, purple pen use, highlighter use, etc.

If you see staff marking books at lunchtime, ignore them and walk by. Don't disturb them. They can eat and mark at the same time. It's all about the books. Think about buying staff a book trolley so they can take books home.

Once you have established the non-negotiables for literacy and maths, roll it out for all books for all subjects. It's unmanageable but for a couple of years, staff will do it. Hopefully, in this time, Ofsted will have been and gone, staff will leave, and you can employ newly qualified teachers. You are then free to roll it out again.

Lesson Structure

One of the biggest challenges you will face as a Head is how differently teachers deliver lessons. This can become a huge problem with your plans to raise standards.

There may be a few teachers who are a little maverick in their approach and think they are doing well. However, you'll soon begin to feel out of control. If you allow teachers to deliver lessons any way they see fit, you will find it hard to control them. The answer to this problem is simple.

Make everyone teach in the same manner. In addition to your non-negotiables, you must introduce a set of guidelines that teachers must adhere to, regarding the delivery of all lessons.

You want the confidence to be able to show any visitor around school, knowing exactly what to expect to see in any classroom. If you can't do this, you run the risk of looking like an amateur. You must have a handle on all lessons.

I strongly suggest you adopt some of these top tips:

1. All pupils must line up single file before entering the class.

2. All teachers must fist-bump their pupils as they enter the class.

3. The learning objective must already be on display.

4. Pupils must respond to written feedback within the first five minutes of the lesson.

5. The teaching assistant must be busy, busy, busy. They should not be photocopying in lesson time.

6. Teachers must deliver a seventeen-minute introduction for all lessons.

7. Learning styles must be weaved into lessons.

8. Three-minute mini plenaries must be planned for.

9. A twelve-minute final plenary must be delivered, and the teaching assistant should write up notes on the working wall.

10. Pupil premium children must be asked questions first.

11. Named lolly sticks are the only way teachers should choose pupils to answer questions (by randomly picking a named lolly stick out of a hat). Insist on a no hands-up policy.

12. All adults in the room must remain standing throughout the lesson. They should circulate the room at least five times.

13. Teachers should randomly choose three pupils during the lesson to explain what they are learning. It's good preparation for Ofsted.

14. Ban all forms of apathy. Pupils must look interested in lessons. Pupils are not allowed to yawn, stare out of the window, fiddle with stationery or roll their eyes.

15. Any live marking that is done must require the pupil to respond with a written comment back within two minutes.

16. The expensive resources you often buy (that teachers don't ask for) must be on display and used at some point in the lesson regardless of the activity.

There are many others, but I think this will give you a good start. You may want to consider giving staff three learning walks to meet these guidelines.

After that, start disciplinary action for anyone who is struggling to keep up.

Observations

Regularly observing staff is one of the most effective ways to monitor teaching and learning. Use it shrewdly and you will be able to take complete control of your staffing concerns.

In the past, you weren't expected to observe any lessons and provide written feedback. Later, performance management kicked in and gave you the opportunity to observe staff once a term.

This was considerably better because you could reinforce who your favourite teachers were by giving them outstanding grades. You knew they would share this with other teachers and create more pressure for the staff who didn't do so well.

Any staff who were causing you problems because they were challenging your ideas, providing negative feedback after their observations was a great way to force them to leave. Sadly, grading lessons is frowned upon now. But...

There is good news.

Learning walks.

Whoever started learning walks needs to be congratulated. What a clever piece of management. If you are unfamiliar with learning walks, they work like this (although feel free to adapt it):

Learning walks enable you to drop into lessons (planned or unannounced) and observe the teacher for around ten minutes or so. Because you are not in there very long, it's hard for staff to say it was an official lesson observation. You may find you can squeeze in a learning walk fortnightly or even weekly.

You can use learning walks to implement all your non-negotiables. Walk into any classroom and you will easily be able to pick out several areas that need improving: from working walls to PowerPoint colours, from learning objective slips to the use of purple pen, from teacher questioning to next steps in books. Basically, use it to pressurise your weaker teachers.

For your compliant and supportive members of staff, walk in, smile and give them the thumbs up as you leave. You may even want to think about giving your favourite teachers a little 'heads up' as to what time you are popping in.

Be discreet though. Don't waste too much time in their classrooms even though they may not be fully implementing your non-negotiables.

It's far better to use the time to put more pressure on staff you don't favour.

Make sure you tell staff learning walks are not formal observations but always give them written feedback in any case.

Type up a sheet highlighting the strengths and weaknesses. Always make sure you have at least three times as many weaknesses on the slip than strengths. Consider calling them, 'Even better ifs...' They sound less intimidating.

The beauty of carrying out regular learning walks is that they keep staff on their toes. The fear they generate cannot be underestimated. They will work later at night and work through lunchtime in order to satisfy your non-negotiables. Teachers, by their very nature, don't like to fail at anything. They care too much.

Constantly remind staff to 'do what they would normally do'. Make learning walks sound friendly with low stakes. But, strategically use them to put pressure on upper pay scale staff and anyone over forty.

Always carry a clipboard with you and make lots of notes whenever you walk into classrooms. This is vital. Write anything - your shopping list if you need to. It helps to focus the teacher.

Of course, for the staff you are friends with, feel free to leave the clipboard outside the classroom. You must hold onto these teachers. You could argue that it's not fair on the others but play the game. Your favourites will appreciate your leniencies.

In addition to walking around with clipboards, ensure you do not smile. The teacher will be very nervous because they know the power you possess and the consequences that await.

Smiling will give the illusion everything is all right. It's not. It will never be all right for particular teachers. Get them out of your school as soon as possible.

Use the learning walk to your advantage. Find anything you can to criticise the teacher for. Anything! A brilliant tactic is to sit with as many different groups as possible. This will upset the teacher's natural rhythm and consequently they will spend the whole time focusing on what you are doing and listening in to your conversations with the pupils.

It will cause anxiety and stress for the teacher and at the same time, stops pupils working. Of course, for your favourite teachers, just sit at the back and smile.

Because your feedback will be informal, they can't really use it against you but the pressure they will feel to conform will be vast.

For your compliant staff, immediately pick out the most articulate and more able pupil in the class and ask them what they are learning. Easy. Make a note of what they say.

For members of staff who you are targeting, pick out the pupil who is least likely to give you the answers you need. Perhaps find several pupils who won't be able to articulate exactly what they are learning (even though they are learning). Use this in the feedback to the teacher.

One of the best strategies after a learning walk is not to give any feedback to the staff for a few days. This creates anxiety and extra stress for those who probably already know what you are going to say. Find time to reassure your favourite teachers they did well. A simple smile, a thumbs up and a 'well done today' as they leave school is normally sufficient.

The most important part of a learning walk is not to tell staff what you are looking for. For example, don't say, 'I will be focusing on your use of questioning.' You won't be able to criticise anything else otherwise. Always keep the focus on absolutely everything and anything. Keep staff guessing.

Anytime you have a visitor to the school, carry out a learning walk. This means you can add at least ten more learning walks in addition to your normal ones. Works a treat.

If you find staff kick back against learning walks or you have a particularly annoying union rep who is putting pressure on you to stop them, consider coaching.

Coaching is brilliant.

Tell staff coaching is professional development. Tell staff that coaching is a way to develop their teaching in a supportive manner. Tell staff that they can have a say in what they want you to focus on.

Tell staff it's a two-way process and it's a positive way to help improve their teaching. Tell staff coaching is definitely not a lesson observation or part of a learning walk.

But. It is.

It gives you the same power to regularly observe and root out staff who are not meeting your high standards or not adhering to your non-negotiables. Always give them double the amount of written feedback with a longer list of 'Even better ifs'. It's great. Very clever. Very effective.

The beauty of learning walks or coaching strategies is you are more equipped to deal with questions from Ofsted. When they ask you what they expect to see before entering a particular class, you can discuss a few concerns you may have. If the teacher does well, you win. If they do poorly, you win. It shows how well you know your staff. Ofsted will be impressed with you.

When they ask you what you are doing about any poor teaching seen, simply show them all twenty-five learning walk feedback slips for any member of staff. It will prove you are supporting staff and trying to improve the school. Easy.

Finally, one of my favourite tactics I use a lot at the moment is to unofficially tell staff what grading they got during the ten minutes you observed them. I know grading has been phased out, but you can still tell them.

For example, use the line, 'I know I can't grade you but in old money, that would have been *requires improvement*. Don't write it down. Just a quick comment and it's there, planted deeply into the teacher's head.

Equally, telling a member of staff their lesson was *outstanding* (unofficially of course) will do wonders to their confidence and help to keep them loyal when things get bad (which they will at some point).

Top tip: catch a pupil yawning. This will give you plenty of ammunition to say the lesson wasn't good enough.

Tell the teacher that apathy in the classroom will not be tolerated and write a support plan if required.

A colleague of mine recently told me how she walks into a classroom, observes the lesson and leaves. Nothing unusual about that you might think.

However, she cunningly returns to the same class ten minutes later. She claims it guarantees to catch the teacher out. Teachers are so relieved you have left the classroom, she informs me, they immediately switch off.

Often, they are found holding a conversation with the teaching assistant, dissecting what just happened. Brilliant. I love this. Perhaps you could try it too.

Learning walks. Use them wisely to become the outstanding leader you've always wanted to be.

Of course, you should seriously consider carrying out mocksteds at least once a term. Staff may be aware that other schools have stopped doing them. That's fine. You just need to call it a different name. Try 'Learning Look Week' or 'In Teaching We Trust Week'. Kick butt basically.

Displays

Long gone are the days where staff would put up their displays a few days before the start of each term in the peace and quiet of their classroom.

If you still have staff doing this, they are probably of a certain age. Static displays are now obsolete (well that's what my boss says).

Working walls are the new fad. You can have as many working walls as you like. But make sure staff have a maths and English working wall at the very least.

Ask the caretaker to put some bigger display boards up to cater for the extra workload working walls generate.

Ensure staff always start with a blank working wall and insist they update them every lesson.

Encourage staff to refer to the working wall at the start of all lessons. Add this to your non-negotiables list.

Demand that staff refer to the working wall at the end of the lesson too.

All display text must be handwritten, and sheets must be stuck up at weird angles. Some pieces of paper should overlap the edge of the displays to make them look trendy and modern.

I suggest giving staff some coloured sugar paper and lots of post-it notes to stick up to show how raw and creative the displays are.

It's important to give the impression that working walls are current and up to date.

Working walls prove to any observer that the children are on a learning journey and makes it very clear what learning has occurred.

They're a fail-safe strategy just in case observed lessons go awry.

I would thoroughly recommend finding some exceptional photographic examples of working walls as a model for your staff. There are plenty on social media sites by keen and enthusiastic teachers wanting to show the world their masterpieces.

I would also allocate some staff meeting time to walk around classrooms with staff and critique everyone's working walls. You'll have to disguise it with the comment, 'It'll be good for us to share ideas,' etc. But in reality, what you are trying to achieve is to disguise an opportunity to name and shame staff who are not putting enough effort into their working walls.

Consider having a colour scheme for each subject working wall so they look uniform around the school. As a result, as children move up through the school, they will associate a particular colour with a subject.

For example, all maths working walls could have a blue border. This will prevent any confusion in each year group regarding where pupils need to look for extra support.

There are so many non-negotiables you can create with your management team to ensure working walls all look similar and uniform across the school. It's worth spending some time writing these out and displaying them in the staff room so there are no excuses.

I would recommend working walls are scrutinised at least fortnightly for maximum policing of the policy. Obviously, support plans must be issued to staff who you have concerns about.

After a term, introduce working walls for other subjects too. For example: spelling, science, topic, computing, RE etc. If staff complain that they have no space in their classroom, tell them to use the windows and doors. Failing that, ask them to split their existing boards into different sections to ensure all subjects are covered.

Every week ask staff to take photographic evidence of their working walls and stick them into books. Again, it's another way to ensure observers see what strategies you have put in place (just in case for any reason, observers miss the working walls during a learning walk).

You will find that some staff will resist working walls and revert back to static displays that are colourful and inspiring. You must be wary of this and stamp your authority as soon as possible. It's usually the more experienced teachers that will try this. They will desperately cling onto any scrap of autonomy they can.

Unfortunately, they don't realise that consistency and conformity throughout the school is key. No one should deviate from the non-negotiables. Nobody.

As for communal displays around the school, that's an easy one.

I would suggest that each member of staff is responsible for two communal displays every half term. Staff will moan. Staff will complain about workload. However, are communal displays something *you* want to do? No. I thought not.

Delegate this responsibility to your deputy. They will want to please you and sort it out exceptionally well. They will organise a super timetable for the year, telling staff where and when displays must be done.

Communal displays must be static displays. You simply can't get away with messy and trendy-looking working walls around school.

Communal displays must show excellence. They must be bright and colourful and ideally, only work from your talented and gifted pupils must be up for all to see.

If this means the same pupils' work gets displayed every year, then so be it. It's all for show. You must prove to visitors that the standard of work across the school is exceptional.

Your display board in your office should have lots of data charts and progress sheets slapped all over it to prove to any important observer you are on top of your game.

However, when a parent wants to meet with you, have a temporary display board full of artwork and writing that you can place in front of it to show them how much you value pupils' work.

Consider something on wheels to make the transition effortless. When parents leave, restore the data and progress sheets display.

Something you may want to consider is to spend a lot of money placing inspiring and motivational quotes on every wall. They look very impressive to visitors. Pupils don't care about them. *They* would rather have work up. But these quotes look quite the thing at the moment.

One school I visited recently only had quotes up around school - no work.

It was great. It looked very professional and very business-like. Make the quotes up if you need to - no one will notice.

Displays – they're all for show; it's all for show. Sort these out and you're halfway there.

Progress

Progress. Everything is about progress. You must prove pupils are making progress.

The first thing you should set up are pupil progress meetings with staff. Ideally, these should be at least half termly or fortnightly for faster results.

Pupil progress meetings are great at piling pressure onto staff. You can use them to interview teachers about how they are going to ensure pupils make good or better progress.

Make sure you do your homework first. Look up recent test data and pick out pupils who should be making faster progress. I would also consider picking some pupils randomly and tell the teacher those pupils need to make even faster progress. They might not need to, but it just keeps teachers on their toes.

Teachers will come to the meeting with an idea of how many pupils should meet the end of year expected standards. Ignore them.

Although they know the pupils better than you, they will play safe. Do not allow this to happen. I would suggest adding between 10-20% onto the number of pupils who they say will meet expectations. They will try the same trick for greater depth. Apply the same rule.

Sadly, some pupils will always struggle to meet expected standards. You know the ones. These pupils must be ignored. Do not allow the teacher to spend quality time with these pupils. Provision for these pupils must be kept to a minimum.

Of course, these pupils need the most support, but they will hold back pupils who have the potential to reach greater depth. Obviously, don't word it like that. You'll think of something sensitive to say I'm sure.

Teachers might give you excuses as to why progress is slow: pupils are not being supported at home with homework, pupils have a negative attitude to school, pupils have low self-esteem, etc. This may be true, but you must not let the teacher give excuses.

The teacher has the class for over twenty hours a week. That's not a lot compared to how much time pupils spend at home, but it's still no excuse.

Absolutely grill each member of staff about pupil premium children. Interrogate them for as long as needed. Start conversations off with words such as: 'Why, When, How, What, Who, Where'.

Teachers will probably just respond with the stock phrase, 'I will support them through quality teaching first.' Do not accept that as an answer. Interrogate. Interrogate. Interrogate.

As you thoroughly discuss each pupil and teacher predictions, make sure you are typing it all up on the teacher's performance management profile page. Let them see you are doing this.

Pupil progress meetings are not casual chats. They are deadly serious, and staff must recognise this. They must be held account for poor progress.

If pupils didn't make accelerated progress in the previous year, explain to teachers that it will be their responsibility to make up the progress. If you have members of staff on the upper pay scale, they *must* make up the progress... and more.

Make this very clear to UPS teachers. It also adds a little more pressure on these teachers and hopefully, they will consider leaving, giving you the option to replace them with NQTs.

Try to hold pupil progress meetings a few days after tests are completed. I would suggest formal tests in writing, reading, maths, spelling and grammar. Tell staff that the data analysis must be typed up within three days of the tests being completed. They must email you the data so you can prepare the pupil progress interrogations.

Staff will give you excuses as to why some of the data is poor. They will say things like: 'This pupil felt ill on the day', 'She lost her confidence and gave up', 'Some questions in the paper had content not yet taught', 'There were too many questions to complete in the time allowed', 'Pupils panicked', etc.

Do not accept any of these excuses. You must pile the pressure on. It's simply not good enough.

I would suggest carrying out book looks on the pupils who haven't done very well in the tests. You could even ask the staff to bring their books to the meeting so you can pick up on things to improve.

Make sure you email staff progress sheets showing how their pupils are doing. Highlight in red those pupils who are not doing well in the tests. You may want to name and shame teachers by placing the sheets on the accelerated progress display board in the staff room.

Teachers will also try to convince you that their teacher assessment is a much better indication of how pupils are progressing. Rubbish. Don't buy that one. Test data is all that matters. It's hard data that you can use to impress observers of the school.

If you have favourite teachers, and you will of course, go a little easy on them in pupil progress meetings. You will want to keep these teachers.

Listen compassionately to their excuses as to why the data is poor. Ask them what their 'gut feeling' is as to how each pupil should have done. Use this to fudge the figures.

Perhaps go through the papers with the teacher and get them to tell you which questions they should have got right. Tell the teacher the tests are only one way to complete a picture of a pupil. Play the game. Fudge away.

Accelerated progress will occur much faster if you start booster groups before and after school. Consider starting these clubs from Year 1. Give them fancy club names such as: Whizz Kids Maths Club, Adventure Book Club, Publishing Club. But, use them to focus on SATs. Pupils must make accelerated progress. Naturally, ask upper pay scale teachers to run them. Consider weekend clubs too.

Any pupils, who are not making sufficient progress in lessons, must miss out on foundation subjects in the afternoon. Ensure staff identify these pupils by 11:30am and send them with their work to the deputy's office at 1:15pm.

Call it 'same day intervention'. It doesn't matter if they miss out on the rest of the curriculum if they make progress in maths and English.

In addition to the above, make sure you invest in a fancy online tracking program. Each subject must have between 20-100 objectives. Each objective should be highlighted in a different colour to show 'not meeting, nearly met, just about met, probably met, has met, working towards greater depth, greater depth and greater than great depth.'

All objectives must be updated fortnightly to show progress. Teachers will forget to do it so you must bring it up in every staff meeting. Name and shame if necessary.

The online tracking software will bear no similarity to the other data you are using across the school, but it's another way to collect data and you can use it if you need to.

If the data looks bad on the online tracking software, manipulate the system. It's easy to do.

Just change how many objectives need to be met before pupils are achieving expectations. The whole thing is a waste of time really, but it's another tool in your toolkit to prove progress is happening.

Obviously, book scrutiny is your friend too for checking progress.

Before you check for progress though, make sure you check all the other measurable things such as correct use of coloured pens and highlighters, learning objectives correctly presented, next steps clearly written, deep marking etc. Then look at progress.

Ensure you write out support plans for staff where you feel progress is too slow. You must insist on accelerated progress throughout the school.

Another clever trick is to introduce cold and hot tasks. These are great at showing progress. But you must encourage teachers to cheat.

For example, before a teacher teaches a unit on story writing, ask the class to write a story first.

This becomes your base line assessment. However, teachers must ensure the subject matter is so uninspiring in order to guarantee terrible writing.

The writing must look poor. Remove word mats and dictionaries. Pupils must have less time to complete the task and teachers should refrain from reminding them of any grammar they have taught. It's called a cold task for a very good reason.

Over the next few weeks you will naturally see amazing progress culminating in an unaided piece of work (hot task) where the class write a story that far exceeds their first attempt.

Teachers should be encouraged to make the hot task super exciting using film stimuli and lots of drama games. Word mats and dictionaries must be used. The progress between the cold and hot task will be extraordinary. Play the game people. Play the game.

Remember, when you are asked how you are improving teaching and learning, you have all of the above to fall back on. Prove your impact.

Prove progress is happening every lesson, every day, every term. You'll be fine.

Evidence

Trust nobody. You must insist that staff provide evidence for everything.

As I have already mentioned, I would thoroughly recommend investing in an online assessment and tracking program for staff to use.

There are hundreds of objectives staff can highlight to show how your pupils are doing. Staff should update the objectives fortnightly. I would call them data drops.

You can log on as an administrator to keep tabs on who is keeping up to date with it. Name and shame those who are behind.

In addition, teachers should upload photos and film footage for each objective for each pupil. You must encourage staff to do this as it provides invaluable proof that pupils are meeting particular objectives. There is usually room for staff to write notes too so they can explain the context behind the photos and films.

It is simply not good enough to take a teacher's word for it. For example, a teacher recently claimed that a pupil could confidently count up and down in 2s, 3s, 4s and 5s. Immediately, I asked the teacher to prove it. She couldn't!

She said she had asked the pupil in class and she made a note of it in her mark book. This is not good enough. I told her to record a film of the pupil counting up and down and for the footage to be uploaded to the assessment and tracking program.

She was furious but if you want to be a good leader, these are the decisions you must make and stick by.

Another teacher claimed several pupils in her class were at greater depth for singing. How did she know? She predictably said she had heard them sing several times. Where was the evidence? She should have known better than that. She was on the UPS too. Shocking. I gave her a warning. The films have now been uploaded so I can see them if I need to.

You may find teachers will complain that nobody looks at the evidence that is uploaded. They are correct. However, if you don't make staff do it, they will be encouraged to exaggerate assessments. You can't afford for data to be inaccurate.

I would strongly consider asking teachers to take and print out photos of any practical lessons. They must be stuck into books. They should aim to get close ups of every pupil looking happy and actively involved in something exciting. Once a month, ask teachers to convert photos to black and white for that extra impact.

Photographs provide excellent evidence that pupils in their class are learning and prove to Ofsted that they are providing a wider curriculum. All photos must be annotated so Ofsted understand the context. You may want to encourage staff to do this at lunch time, so it doesn't interfere too much with marking books after school.

Because staff will have lots of photos and film footage on their tablets, ask them to upload them to the website every Friday before they leave school.

I would suggest they write a small paragraph next to each image to explain to parents what they were learning. It's great proof that your staff are engaging with parents and proves to Ofsted again, how exciting your curriculum is.

The same photos must be uploaded to the school Twitter, Facebook and Instagram pages too.

Before staff indicate whether a pupil is meeting a particular objective with photos and films, the pupil must have been seen doing it three times. Ideally, staff must collect evidence of them doing this each time.

You must insist that any word mats or help sheets are strictly kept out of exercise books. Pupils must be encouraged to use them but keeping them out of books means teachers can say they wrote unaided - perfect evidence in most cases.

If staff indicate that pupils can use dictionaries, please make sure they get photographic evidence.

One school I visited recently filmed children reading a book every six weeks to show progress.

Nobody looked at the films and it took teachers hours to complete. However, you must play the game and I think the evidence it generated was first class. Please encourage staff to do this too.

Ask teachers to stamp INDEPENDENT on every piece of work regardless of the help they give the pupils. Evidence. It clearly shows moderators they completed the work without any help.

Something I like to do is to ask staff to initial every page of every exercise book to show me they taught the lesson. It drives teachers mad but how are you supposed to know who taught the lesson?

To be fair, the class teacher teaches most of the lessons, and it was suggested that only supply teachers need to initial work. But it's easier to make everyone do it.

Remember, every piece of work must have a long, printed off learning objective slip with success criteria on. It's a very good way to show evidence of what the pupils were learning. Yes, Ofsted should be able to tell what they were learning from the work, but the learning objective slip is great evidence that the learning took place. Don't allow pupils to write the learning objective; it can look a bit messy.

A recent member of staff who worked for me (she isn't a teacher anymore – I made sure of that), asked the pupils to write a short, two-word title for each piece of work. You can imagine my reaction.

She claimed learning objective slips and lengthy written out ones weren't for the pupils but for observers of books. She said asking pupils to write a very simple title, cut down on workload for everyone.

Under no circumstances should you allow this. How will the pupils know what they are learning? Evidence. You must make sure you have detailed evidence of the learning in books – every day.

You must think all the time: How does the teacher know what to teach? Can they prove it with a learning objective slip?

For moderation meetings, just ask staff to bring books. Staff might ask why the need to upload evidence on the assessment and tracker program if they only look at books. Just ignore them.

Explain that books will give you the evidence you need for a staff meeting. Tell them Ofsted will want to look at the online evidence (they won't but don't mention that). Tell staff that the next teacher will need to look at the online evidence, even though no one does!

Remember to keep evidence of poor teaching. Write a report every time and make sure teachers receive this feedback. If Ofsted pick up on poor teaching, you can use the feedback as evidence of your support. If Ofsted don't pick up on it, don't mention it.

Remember, if staff use a verbal feedback stamper or write VF, they must annotate it explaining what was said. Evidence.

Ideally, when a teacher talks to a pupil, they must show evidence that it happened.

Pupil voice is becoming quite the thing. Regularly pick out articulate and positive pupils to interview about all aspects of school life. It's a great way to show Ofsted and parents how wonderful the school is.

If you are smart, find time to pick other pupils who will be very honest about their teachers. Interview them at length about how well their teacher is doing. It's more evidence you can use to bully a teacher out of the profession if you need to. Don't show these ones to Ofsted.

Staff Meetings

You must have a staff meeting every week. There will be some weeks when you might not need one but resist the temptation to cancel it. Staff would obviously appreciate the extra time off but if you cancel one, staff might think you are weak. Always have a staff meeting; it's a control thing.

Drag meetings out as long as possible. You should aim to make them last for at least ninety minutes, two hours if you can.

Consider asking a member of staff to take minutes. They should start by recording who is present and who turns up late. At the end of the meeting the minutes should be emailed to everyone.

Of course, you are welcome to turn up late whenever you like. Your deputy will cover for you. Just say you had to deal with a parent.

Staff meetings are an opportunity to lay down the law, remind staff of the non-negotiables and give them feedback from the weekly learning walks.

Explain to staff what they need to do to improve and inform them that more learning walks will be organised for the following week. You must always tell them this but feel free not to do them just to keep them on their toes.

Allow staff to discuss matters from the agenda but already have your decision firmly in your head. It doesn't matter what staff say, or what ideas they generate, stick to your plan.

Sometimes it's a good idea to have new policies already downloaded from Google and printed off ready to give out at the end of meetings, regardless of what alternative ideas were generated.

Stamp out any criticism of your ideas publicly. Make others feel nervous about speaking out in future. Think about increasing learning walks and book scrutinies for members of staff who speak out of turn. They'll soon shut up.

'It is what it is' is the standard stock phrase you must use when challenged about workload.

Explain that it's Ofsted's fault and they all need to rally round and get through the next couple of years together as a team. Tell them that when Ofsted has been, you will back off. But don't. Maintain high levels of workload.

During meetings, always drag out what you want to say for as long as possible, knowing that there will be staff with lots of 'any other business', who will keep the meeting going for at least another hour.

When members of staff ask you why the meetings go on too long, throw it back at them saying that the meeting starts as soon as everyone gets there. There's always one person who is late! Put the blame on them.

Consider doing a whole staff learning walk during one of your meetings - to embarrass the teachers because their displays are not finished, or the classrooms are still untidy from the day. Staff will soon realise you do this, and they will spend more time at lunch times sorting out their classrooms. Works a treat.

Make sure you turn the WiFi off before the meeting so staff can't surreptitiously send messages to each other. In fact, you may want to have a box for staff to place mobile phones in. They can be collected again at the end.

Always quote passages from recent education articles and books. You don't need to have read them, but it always looks good. Display quotes from these books on a PowerPoint. Hopefully staff won't have read the articles or the books so you should be able to wing it. You'll look super professional and people will assume you know what you're talking about.

Use staff meetings to roll out as many new initiatives as possible. Staff might suggest that you should slow down, so they can properly embed new policies and ideas. Ignore them. You don't have time to waste. You must improve the school at any cost. Your impact matters. You must be able to tell advisors all about the things you have introduced. Go for it!

Ban eye rolling in meetings. If you see a member of staff rolling their eyes, immediately bombard them with questions. Embarrass the hell out of them. Consider asking your assistant Head to watch for excessive use of eye rolling in the meetings.

Discipline staff who like to doodle or who are planning lessons. They must give you their full attention. Ask staff to have all notebooks in a position where you can see what they are writing. Again, think about asking your deputy or assistant Head to police this.

Power dress for staff meetings. It's a power thing. Just do it.

You must mention Ofsted at least five times every staff meeting.

Have a bet with your deputy as to how many times you can say 'Ofsted'. My record is fifty-three. My deputy bought me a chocolate bar! This is so important. It gets into the psyche of every member of staff. It will resonate in their subconscious, keeping them fearfully respecting that call.

Fear of Ofsted is crucial if you want staff to work harder and longer than ever before. Of course, we all know Ofsted are trying hard to make inspections less stressful, but staff don't need to know that.

Morning Meetings

One of the best ways to reinforce your role as boss is to ensure staff attend weekly diary meetings. They can be on a Friday or Monday morning. Personally, I prefer Monday when staff are at their busiest.

Ideally, aim to start them around 8:15am to cut directly into their preparation time.

Before the meeting, make sure your deputy has written up important events for the week on the staffroom whiteboard. Of course, staff can read this for themselves without the need for a meeting but that's not the point. The point is, you get to read what's on the board to staff, reinforcing your leadership prowess.

Consider reminding staff of the non-negotiables and mention Ofsted again. You must not start the meeting until everyone is present. Make any latecomers feel guilty by embarrassing them with some awkward questions.

Of course, you may want to be late on occasion yourself so you can enjoy the moment when you walk in and all eyes turn on you. It's another power thing. Remember to power dress.

Feel free to use this time to address anything that arose from the previous staff meeting. Some staff might not be fully engaged because they are anxiously looking at the time; realising they won't be ready for their first lesson. Ignore them. They had Friday evening to get organised for Monday's lessons. That's not your fault.

Behaviour

The first rule of managing poor behaviour is to delegate the management of poor behaviour. It doesn't matter how big or small your school is, you must always avoid dealing with poor behaviour yourself.

The moment you start to get involved with day to day behaviour problems, staff will take it for granted you will support them.

One of the easiest decisions you can make is to stay in your office as much as possible. You may feel the urge to walk around corridors and spend time on the playground. You must resist this urge. The problem is, you will see all sorts of behaviour issues that you will naturally want to deal with.

However, this will take up too much of your time and staff will soon become de-skilled in dealing with these issues. It's just easier to remain invisible. Staff will appreciate the extra responsibility.

At some point, staff will begin to send pupils to you when they have had enough.

To be fair, these pupils often cause lots of problems for the teacher and probably need to be out of class for a while - for the teacher, the other pupils and for the poorly behaved child too.

However, you simply don't have time to get involved with these issues. If staff do send pupils to you, I suggest you do one of three things:

1. Send the pupil back after five minutes (possibly with a bribe to behave).

2. Let them play on your iPad.

3. Send them to another class with a book.

The beauty of delegation is you avoid pupils being sent to you in the first place. Make it very clear to staff there is a chain of command when dealing with poor behaviour.

For example, pupils must be seen by another teacher first. Then, the Key Stage leader can get involved. Finally, the assistant Head or the deputy can intervene. At no stage should *you* be dealing with this.

One way to minimise teachers sending pupils out, is to make staff write out lengthy behaviour slips. Each slip should take at least fifteen minutes to complete and be personally handed in to you. This will deter them from sending pupils out in the first place. Works a charm.

Your time is precious. Keep it that way.

I highly recommend that you keep notes on staff who send pupils to you on a regular basis. Why? Because their teaching is probably not engaging enough which is why the pupils are messing about.

You must put the emphasis back onto staff. On occasion, feel free to use poor behaviour in lessons against members of staff that question your decision making. If staff can't handle poor behaviour, put them on a support plan.

To make the delegation of managing poor behaviour more efficient, introduce a long-winded and complicated behaviour flowchart.

For every poor choice a pupil makes, a member of staff can simply look at the flowchart to find out how best to de-escalate the problem. The flowchart should be so complicated that it almost becomes unusable. Have lots of arrows and 'yes – no' options. Have lots of staggered sanctions on the document.

Of course, the final option should have you as the last resort. However, if you make the flowchart work to your advantage, you shouldn't need to get involved.

I found giving a senior teacher the title 'Behaviour Support Mentor' helped me in the past. Pick someone who wants to make an impression on you or who is very ambitious. They will pick up all the slack and work their socks off for you.

The second rule of managing poor behaviour is you don't talk about poor behaviour.

Avoid discussing it with staff. You must repeatedly tell parents that the behaviour at the school is excellent. It's a massive public relations thing.

Think about going for a kite mark in something like 'Nurturing Pupils Gold' or 'Happy Kids Diamond'. Splash this all over your newsletters.

Off-rolling pupils is one option too. Persuade parents that their child would benefit from moving school for reasons you can improvise. Seriously. Loads of schools have done it. You'll get the idea pretty quickly. It works a treat.

Movement around school must be managed carefully. All children must walk with their walk buddies. Pupils must stay on the left hand side of all stairs and corridors. Ask members of the management team to police pupils walking around the school.

Consider installing CCTV with sensitive microphones to pick up any social chatter. Ideally, you want pupils walking in silence.

Planning

Ofsted have said they are not interested in day-to-day planning. Some teachers will hold you to account if you ask for any. However, there are ways around it.

Staff will be used to mapping out long term plans so just ask them to add lots more information on them. Ensure teachers add key questions, national curriculum links, resources and how it links with other year groups' planning.

Insist that long term plans are written up on the correct template with the school logo and motto on. You must make staff feel a part of the new look, corporate feel. It will give the staff a sense of identity and will help to consolidate your leadership presence.

Ensure the long-term plans are scrutinised regularly and any slight imperfections (font size, colours, grammar) are quickly addressed with that member of staff or year group.

Consider looking at some old long-term plans and ask staff to provide evidence that they delivered what was on the planning.

This is crucial because some teachers will download schemes of work from the internet, not read them and just copy and paste them into long-term plans to satisfy your request for detail. The more experienced teachers are very savvy at this. They know how to play the game. Watch them carefully.

Staff will tell you they find it hard to plan in so much detail for the year ahead, but you must make sure they do in case Ofsted want to see how well you have planned the curriculum. They will want to carry out subject deep dives.

Consider changing the curriculum every year to keep everyone on their toes. Teachers are paid well. They should be able to create new planning year upon year.

Weekly planning is a big issue presently. Some schools say they don't look at them as it's down to the teacher how they plan. Don't believe them. They *will* be checking don't you worry. They are very sneaky. You too, must check weekly planning.

Try to get staff to hand in weekly plans for you to scrutinise. Hopefully, you won't get any resistance. Plans should have the names of all the special needs children in a different coloured font and a list of interventions the teacher is using to teach them.

It makes it obvious that the teacher has thought about their special needs pupils. If a teacher fails to include this on their planning, reprimand them as they clearly don't know how to teach pupils with special needs.

Evidence of assessment for learning must be seen on the planning. Annotations must be scribbled over the plans in order to prove the teacher has successfully evaluated each lesson and shown how to move the pupils on.

You must be very careful when asking to see the annotated plans. Do not give staff time to quickly make it up.

For example, don't ask for annotated plans to be handed in the next day. Teachers will make it up that night (playing the game).

Always surprise staff by asking to see their annotated plans at the beginning of a staff meeting. This will sort out the weak teachers and will immediately tell you who to target for extra learning walks.

If staff complain about this level of scrutiny, just tell them it's good professional development. Tell them how good it is for staff to share and discuss different ways to plan. Tell them it's good for the new teachers to see how it's done. Be smart. The last thing you need are phone calls from unions about it.

Insist that all planning is uploaded to the server. Tell them you check every week to make sure they do it.

Make an example of someone in a staff meeting if anyone fails to comply. It will help to encourage conformity.

The other option for dealing with staff who refuse to plan in detail for you (because they claim they don't have to anymore) is to carry out an extra learning walk. It's easy to pick up on something in their lesson that isn't perfect. Use this against the member of staff and insist they write up detailed plans for you to see.

They won't have a leg to stand on. I can't emphasise enough how important it is to stop lazy staff from cutting corners.

You had to write up detailed plans as a teacher. They should too.

Another strategy, which is becoming very popular with my Headteacher friends, is to ask for all PowerPoint and interactive slides to be uploaded to the server for scrutiny. Can you see how the emphasis isn't on planning?

Instead, the focus is on slide quality. But because teachers over-rely on slides to teach, the slides have become their plans really. Ask to see their slides. Don't mention planning.

The slides will give you a good idea how well they are preparing lessons. Look out for transition effects, animations and a variety of sounds. Staff who add these features to slides will care more about their pupils than those who don't.

In fact, any slides that have white backgrounds should be your first warning sign that the teacher is coasting. You must swiftly deal with this. Start to introduce non-negotiables for slides. Start off by insisting that all slides must have the same coloured background.

Then add little extras like what font the learning objective must be on the slide, where the school logo must appear, the size of the fonts and what type of questions must be evident.

Look out for slides that are out of date. Look at when slides were created and modified on the server. Discipline staff who are just digging out old slides.

If you see a Twinkl logo on any slide, you must take immediate action.

I suggest putting a member of staff, who is seen using a Twinkl PowerPoint, on a support plan. Staff will beg you to let them use these slides as they claim it saves them hours of preparation.

But this is a clear sign of laziness and teachers who do this need to be firmly spoken to. I had nothing like this in my day and I turned into an outstanding teacher and Headteacher (according to my partner).

Be brave. Staff will thank you for it in the long run.

Middle Leaders

Play this right and your workload will reduce dramatically.

You have a deputy Head who is keen to become a Head. You have an assistant Head who wants to be a deputy Head. Delegate as much as possible. That goes without saying.

However, try to get lots of other staff on the 'middle leaders' bandwagon.

Tell a handful of unsuspecting teachers they can go on a middle leader's course.

Watch, as their egos inflate with pride and joy. They will be on the phone to their friends and family, telling them of their new promotion. But of course, it isn't. You don't have to pay them anything extra, just promise they can have a day's release now and again to get the work done. They'll forget about that promise eventually.

But if they do remember, make up an excuse about budgets being tight and explain that's what middle management is all about.

Challenge their commitment if they complain further. Because they are middle management, feel free to dish out jobs like risk assessment monitoring for trips, organising residentials, extra break duties, unpaid lunch duties, running more clubs etc. They will love it. By the time the novelty has worn off, you'll be long gone.

You must insist anyone who was on the UPS when you started, get the hardest and most time-consuming jobs around the school. Invent new jobs if you need to. UPS staff will very quickly drain your pitiful budget. The quicker you can encourage them to leave, the better. Everyone is doing it.

Any slight imperfection in their teaching, come down heavily on them. Support plans normally do the trick, and most will resign within a term. Remember, your enthusiastic middle leaders are ready to take over their roles.

Remember to tell middle leaders not to discuss with staff conversations you might have with them. Encourage them to silence any negativity in the staffroom and insist they feedback exactly which teachers are complaining in private.

Allocate a middle leader to check all social media activity amongst the staff to ensure teachers are not moaning about you. WhatsApp groups must be banned if possible. If this proves too difficult to manage, you must monitor WhatsApp activity immediately after a staff meeting. This is when staff are most active.

Of course, you must have your own middle leaders' WhatsApp group so they can be contacted any time of day or night. They will feel very privileged and will help to massage their egos further. Use the group to increase their workload when appropriate. Strategically increase the workload over the year. Perhaps map it out so the increase is almost unnoticeable.

I would also set out rules for social media activity. Ask middle leaders to police this too. Any photos staff upload to their own social media accounts must follow the guidelines below.

1. Skirts must fall below the knees

2. Absolutely no cleavage must be on show

3. Tattoos must be hidden

4. Beards must be trimmed and look tidy

At the end of the year, reward your middle leaders with a certificate. It means nothing but it will help to maintain their enthusiasm for the second year.

Remind them that Ofsted like a school with middle leaders. Repeatedly tell your middle leaders how important their role is in the school. Reduce your workload and responsibility wherever possible.

Communication

You must promote a healthy work life balance for your staff.

Send emails to staff in the evening and at weekends when they have more time to read them. The school day is busy enough without staff having to read their emails during lessons.

You may find some teachers will complain about emails being sent in the evening and at weekends, but you can easily get around this by writing 'Not to be opened until after 7pm' on the email.

It publicly shows you care about any home commitments they may have and will stop the pressure to read emails straight after work. This way, staff will know they have a few hours grace after work to relax first.

Think about writing a Headteacher's Bulletin every weekend and sending it to staff on a Sunday night. Sunday night is when teachers are often working so they are more likely to read it.

On it, highlight what books you will be scrutinising, how many learning walks you will be doing and include polite reminders about classroom environments and how best to deal with behaviour issues.

I find the bulletin encourages staff to start the week in the right frame of mind and pumps them full of adrenaline, ready to cope with their workload.

I also find it very helpful to test teachers in staff meetings about the latest bulletin. Pick a member of staff and ask them questions about it. Have they read it? You'll know if they haven't. Repeat this with as many members of staff as you need to until staff get into the habit of reading the bulletin.

I suggest addressing children as 'learners' in the bulletin. Always refer to children as 'learners' when you are talking to staff. It clearly shows you are thinking about learning all the time. Don't call them pupils or students. That's old fashioned now.

Use the bulletin to praise your favourite teachers too.

Obviously use it to remind staff what they need to do to improve.

Mention Ofsted a few times to keep them alert and focused.

The staffroom whiteboard is a crucial tool in communication. Make sure you get a middle leader to update the board every day. On occasion, you might forget to ask them to add something to the whiteboard. Don't worry, sneak in just after registration and add it yourself.

When staff say they didn't know about the said message, tell them they must read the board more carefully as you wrote it up at 7:30am. Do not admit you got it wrong.

Use the school's text messaging service to full effect. Ask the office to send out at least one text message to staff every day with reminders etc.

After all, teachers have their phones on them all day, so this is a great way to communicate with staff.

Tell staff to have their phones on vibrate so they are always aware that school is contacting them. They should double check their phones at break and lunch times. Encourage them to do this at the same time they are checking their unread emails from the night before.

I am currently trialling video phone calls with staff when I need something urgent done. It's great. Insist that staff have this feature activated on their phones so you can have that face to face conversation when you need to. Ideally, try to make the calls after 7pm to give staff a chance to unwind after work.

Install phones into all rooms to save office staff from having to walk to classes. It disrupts lessons all the time, but it makes life easier for the office staff and means they can spend more time working for you.

Consider telling staff they must answer the class phone during the first five rings to avoid any lesson time wasted.

If you have the money, invest in walkie talkies for all the staff. They can be clipped onto their belts and means they can be contacted during the day, wherever they might be. You must be able to contact staff all the time. This means they can't use the excuse, 'I didn't know'.

Whenever you feel under pressure with work, simply use the 'out of office' standard email reply. Keep this on for a few weeks until you catch up.

Encourage staff to write weekly class bulletins for parents, write what the pupils are doing for the day on a playground easel and update blogs and the website every week. Parents must be informed all the time. You must keep parents onside. It adds to teacher workload but it's worth it.

Every teacher must set up a class Twitter and Facebook page and upload photos and notices on Mondays, Wednesday and Fridays.

Regularly update the teacher handbook of rules and non-negotiables so there is no excuse for staff forgetting them. Email this to staff at least fortnightly.

A colleague of mine employs his fourteen-year-old son to place reminder leaflets on staff cars after work. His son says it's better than having a paper round and pays more. It might be something to consider for the future. I have personally used this method for giving lesson observation feedback if I have been in a rush. Use petty cash to keep it under the radar.

You will probably experience a lot of staff absence so it's imperative that you find the right bank of supply teachers.

They must be fully aware of your ambitious plans for the school. Supply teachers must fully support this.

Therefore, ask new supply teachers to arrive for a 7am morning induction meeting on their first day.

During the session, you can talk through the non-negotiables and marking policy.

Let them know that you expect them to work through lunchtime and to still be at work until at least 5pm.

Make it clear to them that the first day is a probation day only. Explain that you will give them written feedback that evening and if successful, they will be invited back.

Whenever the same supply teacher works in a different year group, you must make them attend another 7am morning induction meeting.

Communication with staff is crucial. It's just good leadership.

New Policies

Once you have established areas of weakness across the school, you must introduce your new policies as quickly as possible.

For staff to feel like they are part of the process, allow them time to discuss new ideas over a few weeks. Place sugar paper up in the staffroom for staff to write up ideas during lunch times. Expect every teacher to contribute at least three ideas.

Ask staff to fill in idea sheets and write on post it notes during staff meetings.

Consider asking middle leaders to introduce new policy ideas to take the pressure off you. However, you must already know what the policy will look like before you start these proceedings.

Have the non-negotiables clearly mapped out. Know them inside out.

It is important that you give the illusion of ownership of these policies through discussions and debate, but the truth of the matter is, you will have already decided.

Hopefully, you can cleverly steer the conversation towards what you really want. But even if you can't, just introduce your policy anyway. Tell staff you have thought long and hard about their ideas. Congratulate them on wanting to improve the school as 'it's their school after all'. Tell them they should feel proud of wanting to improve the school etc.

Have the new policy document all printed up and signed off by the governors ready for the last staff meeting on it. Try not to be all 'Blue Peter' about it – 'here's one I made earlier', but you get the idea.

Staff must feel like they own the policy, but in reality, you have already written it. It's tricky, but you'll soon get the hang of it.

Sometimes, you can just download another school's policy document, change the logo and you have your new policy done and dusted. Easy.

If you are really focused, consider not allowing staff to discuss new policies. Just tell them. Consider giving the policy fancy names such as 'Wizard Writers School Handbook' or 'Steps to Success in Science'. But basically, they contain all of the rules teachers must adhere to in order to implement your plans.

Be ready to put staff on support plans if they don't implement your policies quickly and effectively. There must not be any deviation from the policies. All staff must do the same. You are striving for everything to be identical across the school from books and displays to lessons and data.

Staff will tire of your new policies but stay strong. They can always leave and find jobs elsewhere. Your job is to raise standards, not to address pupil and staff wellbeing and workload concerns.

Staff Management

Newly qualified teachers need to be very carefully managed.

They will be full of enthusiasm. They will have lots of new and exciting ideas. They will be social media savvy and be completely up to date with current trends and fads. They may even be aware of some schools who have massively reduced their marking policy and stopped lesson observations.

Even worse, they may have been sucked into teaching believing the teaching recruitment adverts were a true representation of what teaching is like. They will struggle.

They need to be moulded and forced to become the teachers you want them to be. They must buy into your vision. You will be under pressure for books and lessons to look identical, so it is imperative that the new teachers are monitored closely. They will probably struggle with your expectations, but you must persevere.

Some NQTs may leave by Christmas or certainly by the end of the first year. You may be lucky. They may hang around for a couple of years. They won't have the luxury you had as an NQT - complete autonomy to develop as a teacher. They must fall into line. Quickly. They must perform as well as your most experienced teachers within a few weeks.

NQTs are unlikely to contact their unions so you have quite a lot of wriggle room to pile the pressure on.

The upper pay scale was introduced as a way to reward teachers who were good at their job but didn't necessarily want to be part of the management team. It was a nice sentiment, but times have changed. The fact of the matter is, you don't have the funds to pay for this anymore. You may have several teachers on the UPS. This is a big problem.

Often, these teachers are good at managing their workload, make the job look easy and have a great relationship with the parents and pupils.

The problem is they will also speak up and confront your policies, picking holes in your decision making.

Although this can be incredibly irritating, you can use this irritation to your advantage. Somewhere in the UPS policy it states teachers must make a substantial and sustained contribution to school. And there it is. A very woolly statement that you can manipulate.

Start giving these teachers extra jobs. Start expecting lessons to be outstanding all the time. Insist they run lots of clubs and cover lunch duties. When they complain, challenge the fact they are not meeting the standards for UPS pay.

Threaten UPS staff with support plans. The pressure will very quickly get to these teachers. They will feel confused. They will feel angry and probably contact their unions. But unless you have handled things very unprofessionally, a union rep can't do very much. Be transparent and as professional as possible.

To show how much you care, send some of these teachers to other schools to observe better teachers. On paper, it looks like you are doing everything possible to support your staff. They get out of your hair for a day and they will feel humiliated as they reluctantly arrive at their support school. It works well. Try it.

To maximise extreme pressure, target staff who challenge you the most, first. They will either go off long-term sick or leave. The ripple effect amongst staff is powerful. They soon become aware of the consequences of speaking up. Consider increasing your staff sickness insurance.

Schools across the country are implementing this strategy so don't feel guilty. Unions are taking on more staff to deal with the UPS issue so support will be there for these teachers if required.

Make sure you big-up the other teachers who are just plodding through their day on the teacher main scale. They will have seen how you deal with non-conforming staff and will be nervous.

Make sure you praise them publicly when possible otherwise you will have too many staff off sick and it becomes unmanageable.

For all staff, ensure you use the triangulation technique for performance management. This is crucial if you want to maintain high standards from staff and gives you plenty of ammunition to put staff on support plans.

If you are not aware of how triangulation techniques work, don't worry, many Heads don't, or refuse to use it. I will guide you through it.

Firstly, choose three areas in which teachers must excel in over the year. I always suggest the following:

- Observations / learning walks
- Books
- Data

Using this technique means you can very easily pick one area that isn't quite as strong and use it against the teacher.

They may argue that they do a fantastic job but tell them it's the 'triangulation of evidence' that is inconsistent, and it's this reason why they are being put on a support plan or having their pay frozen.

You may want to consider extending the triangulation technique to four or five areas. Just make sure you give it a fancy name.

Something you might want to consider is modelling a performance management review for a teacher so other leaders can learn from your approach.

Invite your deputy and middle leaders to attend. Model how brutal you must be in these meetings. Ask them to make notes and debrief the meetings with them afterwards.

Once they are fully trained, they will be able to take over your role, leaving you more time to do other things. They will enjoy the extra responsibility. Easy.

It is standard now for all staff to wear a lanyard. Controversially, ask your governors if you can place tracking devices on the lanyards.

From the luxury of your office, you can monitor the percentage of lessons teachers spend sat down. The software will provide step counts and hot spots where staff spend most of their time.

You'll need to approach this one sensitively but it's a brilliant piece of kit and the stats you can pull from it are remarkable. You will very quickly get a feel for who your lazy teachers are. It provides conclusive evidence they are not trying hard enough to engage with the class.

With so many teachers interested in teaching pedagogy, they will attend professional development sessions at weekends run by teachers up and down the country. They will buy books on teaching and will constantly look to further improve their teaching.

They are wasting their time.

Are you going to allow your staff to start experimenting with new ideas and fancy fads? No. They must all do the same thing, dictated by you.

You may want to tell staff they don't need to take a personal interest in improving their teaching. They should be encouraged to do what you tell them to do. After all, you know best.

I once allowed a member of staff to watch her son's first sports day during lesson time. Big mistake. I was inundated with requests to do the same. Some teachers didn't even have children!

It's just easier to say no to all staff when they request time off to watch their own children in a school event. You will have to toughen up a bit I am afraid.

CCTV is relatively cheap nowadays. Think about installing it everywhere. Tell staff it's to deter people from breaking into the school. However, use it to stop talking in the corridors, to monitor the quality of teaching and see which teachers leave classrooms for last minute photocopying.

Set up some surveillance monitors in your office, make a cup of tea and watch away.

Staff Sickness

Staff absence can be a big problem in schools. Some teachers will have the odd day off and others will be off long term.

Teachers might self-certificate for a few days or they may beg for a sick note from the doctor for a few weeks. Some staff will notoriously have time off around busy periods (report writing and Christmas).

How you respond to staff absence is crucial. Handle it naively, and you will experience excessive staff sickness. Handle it right and you will deter staff from having time off in the first place.

Mobile phones have made it all too easy for staff to send a text message informing school of their sickness. Under no circumstances should you allow staff to do this. It's just too easy to do. You must make staff phone in sick. This alone, can be enough to put teachers off having a day at home.

However, you will soon notice that teachers will start asking their partners to phone in on their behalf. This again, must not be tolerated. It makes it all too easy to stay off sick. You must insist the person who is claiming to be sick, is the one responsible for phoning in. The extreme anxiety this generates will almost certainly make teachers think twice.

Unfortunately, you will come across other, more determined staff, who will play the game confidently and be quite happy to phone in personally. They will have devised a routine of how to do it too.

In order to make their voice sound different, they will probably lay down in bed as they make their call. They may even pinch their nose to exaggerate their symptoms. You may have an inkling they were going to call because they often mention how rough they are feeling the day before.

Choose a middle leader to receive all sick calls. Choose this person very carefully as they need to have an element of fear about them. Staff should feel nervous talking to them.

Ensure you train up your middle leader carefully. They must know what to say depending on the reasons given by the member of staff.

For example, if someone calls in sick with a cold, the following questions must be asked:

1. On a scale of 1-10, how rough do you feel?

2. Do you think you will be in tomorrow?

3. Have you taken any paracetamol yet?

4. Where is your planning?

They must be told to phone the school again at lunch time with a further update call at the end of the day. They must also email any recent written assessments from previous lessons to help the supply teacher make accelerated progress during the day.

Any to-do lists must also be emailed in so their workload can be shared around the staff to complete.

If the member of staff reports for duty the following day (which they normally do because they don't want the hassle), you must make them attend an 8am back-to-work interview where you can interrogate them regarding their absence.

In the unlikely event they have more than one day off, follow the same procedures every day but for every day off, add an additional thirty minutes to the back-to-work interrogation interview. I would also advise that you ask your assistant Head to attend the meetings to take notes (they don't need to, but it adds a little more tension to the meeting).

If you have a member of staff signed off for a few weeks, it's crucial you don't personally contact them otherwise you might have their union complaining. However, you can get around this by tapping up one of their closest friends in school. Get *them* to contact the sick person with some questions. Find out when they are likely to return etc.

If a member of staff has more than two weeks off work, you must start disciplinary procedures against them.

I usually call them Stage 1, 2 and 3, increasing in severity for each step. You simply can't have teachers off long term with stress just because of your management style.

For every two weeks they have off, request a meeting with them to discuss their wellbeing. Suggest that maybe teaching isn't for them. Let them know there are small financial packages available if they want to leave quickly (as long as they sign the whistle-blowing contract). Believe me, it's cheaper than paying sick cover for a year or more.

In a recent case, I put a member of staff on a support plan the day they went off sick. It made it much easier to get rid of them. It just added to their stress and made it very difficult for them to want to return. I paid them two months' salary and employed an NQT within weeks.

Also, consider adding a video phone call section to your sickness policy. Put it in the small print. This will enable you to make a video phone call to the person who is sick (whether they're off for one day or several months).

129

Cleverly write it so you have permission to make this intrusive video phone call in order to assess their condition. If a member of staff doesn't answer the call, they will be in breach of their contract.

I've not had a member of staff call in sick now for three years. Although, lots of staff do resign.

Sadly, there may be other reasons why staff call in sick. The death of a pet often comes up. Or even more tragic, a family member becomes gravely ill or even dies. You must be sensitive in this situation as unions will have a field day if you get this wrong.

However, there are a few questions you can ask to check if they are telling the truth:

1. How close were/are you to the person?

2. Were/Are they part of your immediate family?

3. On a scale of 1-10, how sad do you feel?

4. Do you think you will be in tomorrow?

If they hang up, you know it's a genuine call. If, however, you get lots of 'erms and ers' you know they are faking. You'll be surprised what staff will say to get a day off!

Staff Wellbeing

Staff wellbeing is very topical at the moment.

Staff knew the job would be hard when they signed up but in recent years, there's been a lot of social media attention on staff wellbeing. It's a pain to be honest and you will need to manage it sensitively.

Apparently, Ofsted are beginning to look at how well a school looks after its staff. Play the game. Give the impression you care about their wellbeing. Here are a few suggestions.

1. Always say to staff, as they leave the building with a suitcase of books, 'Have a lovely weekend.' Show you care.

2. Put a wellbeing poster up in the staffroom reminding staff it's only a job and to ensure they have hobbies etc.

3. Organise a termly yoga session with Mrs Sunshine. Make this compulsory.

4. Make sure you buy some cheap biscuits and doughnuts every few weeks. Always leave a card with the message, 'I really appreciate you all working 60 hours a week.'

5. Regularly remind teachers how lucky they are to get thirteen weeks holiday - plenty of time to recover and unwind.

6. Offer counselling with yourself (make sure you complete the ten-minute online training first – it's only £25). Nobody has taken up my offer yet, but at least I tried.

7. Deflect workload by repeatedly telling staff when Ofsted has been and gone, you will ease off. You won't of course, but it helps address wellbeing in the short term.

8. Walk around the school at least once a week telling staff they really should go home. I usually do it at 4:30pm as I leave. They might grunt at you because they will be updating their working walls and marking their books. But again, at least you've tried. Tick that wellbeing box.

9. Have some relaxing rainforest music on loop in the staff toilets. Teachers often go there to cry so it's always a good place to have it playing.

10. Reduce emails to only ten a day and make sure they are sent after 7pm to avoid intruding on family time.

11. Weekend emails must only be sent on Sunday evenings when staff are more likely to be working.

12. Send wellbeing questionnaires home for staff to complete. They must not take more than an hour to fill in. Ask staff to answer one every half term. They prove you care.

13. Fudge any negative questionnaire results before handing them in to the governors (goes without saying).

14. Ban teachers talking negatively in the staffroom. Spread the message that negativity and criticism upsets other teachers. It also helps to stop staff rebelling against you. Keep them in line.

15. Finish one or two staff meetings on time.

16. Buy stress balls or fidget spinners for all members of staff.

17. Offer staff a free flu jab (but make sure it's done on a Friday in case they start to feel unwell).

18. Some schools have bought wellbeing dogs as school pets. It's a lot of hassle to be honest. Buy a school gerbil instead. I'm sure it will help in the same way. Cheaper too.

Homework

I'll be honest. Homework is one of the best ways to ensure children succeed in their SATs and other exams.

Pupils should do homework every night. Your reputation is at stake. Ideally, scrap any creative topic homework tasks such as, 'Make a Roman shield'. These tasks will not do. They must always be linked to literacy and maths.

Make sure all homework relates to test style questions to give pupils a head start leading up to exams and tests.

Staff must mark all homework within two days of it being handed in. They must give written feedback and ensure pupils respond to it. Make sure staff keep on top of homework. They must upload homework to the school website so there's no excuse for pupils not to do it.

Consider signing up to numerous maths and literacy websites so pupils can do homework online. Tell staff to set up usernames and passwords for all the pupils and to personalise the homework for each class. They must monitor how the pupils do and regularly assign new tasks. It adds to their workload but that's how teaching is at the moment.

Any pupils who fail to complete homework must miss all their breaktimes until they have completed it. Tell staff to email parents too, explaining the importance of homework and how it helps to meet school exam targets.

Name and shame pupils who don't complete homework. It sounds harsh, but teachers only have a few hours a day to make an impact. It's just not enough time. Pressure must be maintained on children to do work at home. You won't regret it. Children might be more stressed, but it will ease the pressure on your data.

Always send homework out over the holidays. It will help give your school the edge over other schools.

Classroom Environment

You must dictate what the environment is like in every class. It's a great way to reinforce your leadership - a tool to prove your impact and give you complete control over how things need to be done.

I always like to start with colours. Working wall displays must be the same colour throughout the school. PowerPoint slides must be the same colour and mounted work must use the same coloured paper. It seems unnecessary but it helps to make the school look more corporate, neat and super consistent.

Every class must have the same pencil pots. Staff might not like it, but it helps to create that uniformity you are striving for. Each pencil pot must have the same stationery inside. I always suggest the following:

Glue stick, pencils, purple pens, rulers, highlighters, pens and a pair of scissors. It's up to you really. Just make sure it's the same in every classroom.

Teachers will probably resist this policy because they will have their own way of doing things. However, if you start letting them decide on how best to store pencils, what else will they want to do? Don't risk it.

You must also dictate the seating arrangement for all classes. For maths, children must sit in rows and be mixed ability. Always. It's quite the fashion. Don't get left behind.

For literacy, teachers must move the tables back again so children can sit in groups. They must be in ability groups on Mondays and Wednesdays and mixed ability groups on the other days.

During other lessons, children must sit in a horseshoe arrangement. It looks nice and is one of my favourites. I think you will like it too. Make staff do this in the afternoon.

Introduce learning walks to ensure seating plans are being adhered to for each lesson.

I have already mentioned the importance of working walls. Just make sure that the non-negotiables list for the displays is up to date.

Every class must have interactive areas where children can play with artefacts and objects and respond to questions written out by the teacher. Pupils won't have any free time to do this of course, but insist they are on display because it will look good for visitors.

The same applies for reading corners. They look great and give the impression that teachers are promoting reading. Ensure pupils do not sit in the reading corner because they mess about too much. Restrict any pupil changing their book to thirty seconds. That's plenty of time to get in and get out again. Reading corners make the classroom look cosy too.

Whole school targets must be on display - preferably somewhere where visitors can clearly see them. It's another way to prove you are actively on top of moving the school forward. It looks very boring and does nothing to help pupils. Play the game.

I often put my whole school targets up in the staff toilets to remind teachers what they are. Also, it guarantees Ofsted will see them.

An example of whole school targets that could be displayed:

1. Increase boys' attainment in writing

2. Increase greater depth percentages

3. Manage low level behaviour more effectively

Spot check classrooms to make sure teachers have these up within the first few days of term. Make sure you point them out when you are showing visitors around the school.

Growth mindset is a big thing in schools. Keep up with it if you can. I recommend you print off some Twinkl posters and ask staff to put them up somewhere in class. The 'I can't do it…yet,' seems to be very popular. Go with this one first.

Once up, staff can ignore them and go back to focusing on the whole school targets sheet and the trendy working walls.

Visual timetables must be evident on all four walls to help reduce pupil anxiety. It means staff can walk around the classroom and a visual timetable will always be in view for pupils.

Ask staff to make the pictures drab and black and white. If they look too colourful and exciting, they will distract the children from their learning.

All classrooms must have a visualiser, a stand-up easel, a wall mounted white board and an interactive whiteboard. Teachers must utilise all of them for every lesson. Definitely add this to your non-negotiables list. Use learning walks to make sure this happens. Staff must be put on support plans if they are not using these resources. They are not cheap.

All classrooms must have a learning objective area. This is a space where the teacher can write up the learning objective using the school's agreed handwriting style. The learning objective must also be typed up on the interactive board so pupils can see it in computer font.

Every pupil must have access to five coloured paper cups. They can be easily stacked and sit upside down in front of each pupil. Throughout the lesson, pupils should be encouraged to change the top cup to a different colour to show how they are feeling about their learning.

For example:

Red: I don't understand

Orange: I sort of understand

Yellow: I understand but need some help

Blue: I get it but keep an eye on me

Green: I understand completely

Teachers should scan the room every two minutes and immediately address the learning of all the pupils depending on what colour cup is showing. Teaching assistants must also have a set of cups to show you how *they* feel about how the lesson is going. It's immediate feedback and will help staff improve their lessons.

Pupils must not fiddle with the cups, throw them on the floor, poke holes in them, draw on them, place them on their head, make fake breasts with them or pretend they are fake ears. Teachers must nip this in the bud very quickly.

All classrooms must have a list of their pupil premium children on display and an explanation describing how the teacher will teach them. It makes it so obvious to visitors that every single member of staff is addressing pupil premium children. It's a little embarrassing for those children but it is what it is at the moment.

Wet play games such as Connect 4, Top Trumps, Lego and a box of cars and animals must be removed from all classes. All wet play games must be linked to objectives from the curriculum.

I always suggest spelling and times table games. The pupils won't play them but if they do, it will help teachers in the long run. Pupils will soon get bored and be forced to play them.

Encourage teachers to reward pupils with dojo points or house points if they are seen playing the games. Believe me, every little helps.

Tell staff they must not use washing lines to hang work on. They look scruffy and some teachers will go to town with them. There's nothing worse than walking into a classroom where you have to permanently duck. They look messy and they are a distraction to the pupils. Tell staff they keep setting off the fire alarms. That usually works.

To make the classrooms look more office-like, ban the use of blu tack on the walls. Display material must only be put on the working walls. Every working wall must have the school motto visible.

I thoroughly recommend you police teachers' desks or workstations. Teachers must set an example. Mugs and phones are completely banned.

They must be confiscated from staff if you see them out on display. Think about rewarding pupils if they grass the teachers up. It's pretty easy to set up. They love grassing up their teacher. Even better still, ask the pupil to quickly grab the teacher's phone and bring it immediately to you.

All drawer labels must have the agreed font, size and colour. Each label must have a border and the school logo on the top right hand side. The labels must be laminated and stuck on neatly. Encourage staff to use a small spirit level to ensure consistency in straightness.

Every couple of weeks walk around all the cloakrooms and pick up all the jumpers and PE bags. Dump them in the classrooms and directly stare at the teacher as you moan about the mess to the class.

Remind teachers after school *they* are responsible for this mess and add it to the list of things to check on a learning walk. It's embarrassing when visitors walk around. It looks bad on you. Nip it in the bud.

Parents' Evening

I strongly suggest you have a six-weeks-in parents' meeting, another one in November and a final one in the summer term. This is in addition to termly written reports. Staff will complain that this is excessive, but communication with parents is crucial.

Parents' evenings always last longer than expected. Therefore, I would recommend that all consultations are at least fifteen minutes long. This way, teachers will have time to discuss everything they need to, without the pressure of falling behind. Ask the caretaker to lock up after the last consultation at 11pm.

Staff must inform parents of recent test scores, teacher assessments and predicted grades for the end the year. Parents will want to know how their child has settled into the new year and if they are behaving etc. You must train your staff to bypass this as quickly as possible.

Teachers must bombard parents with target setting and data.

It's very much a partnership with parents. They must realise the pressure the school is under and climb on board with targets and testing. Parents must understand that their child needs to be greater depth by the end of the year.

As part of the off-rolling program you may want to persuade parents of children, who are unlikely to meet expectations, that your school isn't for them. Ask teachers to explain that the school doesn't have the resources to meet their needs and the school down the road has. With any luck, you will lose a handful of pupils overnight.

Always make sure you look very busy on parents' evening to discourage parents talking to you. Offer to make staff tea and coffee at least twice throughout the evening.

This way, you impress staff with your apparent kindness, and it allows you to avoid those tricky parents.

Ask a middle leader to stand in the front entrance to deal with any problems. It'll be a good learning opportunity for them.

Ask another middle leader to recruit new pupil premium children. Have a recruitment poster up in the front entrance. Try the headline, 'Are you disadvantaged? Sign up here.' It works particularly well. Bribe parents to sign up by offering a free MacDonald's voucher for four. You can easily raise thousands of pounds for the school. There will be so many parents lingering around.

You must always have a staff meeting the same week. You will have a lot to discuss and you can't afford to miss one. Clubs should not be cancelled either. Parent consultations can easily start after them. You must keep parents happy. If you start cancelling clubs, they will complain.

Ask teachers to write up detailed notes from every consultation and email them to you the same evening. Any parents who fail to turn up, must be contacted by staff within twenty-four hours and a report written up and emailed to you, explaining the reasons for their absence.

Teachers should then arrange a home visit so the important information about targets and test data can be relayed to parents.

Recruitment

Recruiting the right staff is very important. You must make the adverts as attractive as possible. Some of the tricks of the trade can be found below:

1. Don't use the title 'Teacher'. Use a title like 'Educational Director of Classroom Learning'. It sounds much better.

2. Lure ambitious teachers to apply by adding in promises of more money 'for the right candidate'. It will increase applicant numbers but of course, you don't need to pay them more money, even if they are the right candidate.

3. Promise a laptop and an iPad. But, give them old ones that don't really work to save you money. You have kept your promise.

4. Mention things such as 'supportive management team', 'small classes' and 'guaranteed PPA time'. Once they have signed the contract, you can very easily change any of them. They probably won't even remember what was promised on the advert anyway.

5. Mention competitive salary. It's just normal teacher pay scale but it sounds better.

6. Always state you are looking for outstanding teachers. This deters anyone who thinks they aren't. Easy. Only the arrogant and confident teachers apply.

I would make use of drone footage because everyone is doing this at the moment.

You could ask the whole school to stand on the field and make the shape of a phrase like 'This School Is Good – Work Here!' It takes a little bit of organising but it's well worth it.

Use the same drone to film a fly-by of the school, showing off all the outdoor facilities. People like a good drone fly-by. It makes your school look very cool indeed.

Consider making a recruitment film. Study how the government make their adverts to increase teacher recruitment. Do the same for your school.

Set up some fake lessons where you ask a very smiley teacher to teach a funky science task involving a bottle of coke and mentos sweets to six well-behaved pupils. Bribe the pupils to smile incessantly and constantly look amazed and in awe of their teacher.

Ask a few of your mates to pretend to be parents of the school. Film them talking positively about the school.

One of the other tricks that a lot of fellow Heads are using, is to ditch the traditional school sign outside school. Instead, they are spending money on huge, silver-plated lettering that they place high up on the school building. It looks very impressive – almost business like. It's basically stating, 'Our school is highbrow and really posh'. It's not, but it seems to be the thing schools are doing. It's another trick that might help you recruit.

There is another way to recruit but you must be smart about it. Ask your friends and family first if they want a job. I bet they'd love to work with you. They will be dirt cheap.

You won't have to spend money on advertising and an interview lunch for the whole staff. As long as they are DBS checked, you'll be fine.

Good recruitment is all about how well you play the game. It's all about teachers having a positive perception of the school. The reality is usually very different but that's ok. Once your new staff are settled in, you can do what you like. There's not a lot they can do.

Employing a good personal assistant early on is crucial in your success. You may have to let a few teaching assistants go to fund it, but it's worth doing. Teachers will have to cope.

Reports

The longer the reports are, the better. Communication is key. I suggest each report is at least four pages long. Each report should be around a thousand words in length. Make sure the font size is no bigger than 8 to ensure staff write a lot. You are aiming for each report to take about two hours to write.

You must ban the use of copying and pasting. Staff will argue that there's nothing wrong with copying and pasting if the comment is relevant for that pupil. However, what if the parents share reports? They won't be happy.

Some Heads are slimming down their reports by adding more tick boxes to show attainment and progress. Please don't do this. It's lazy and looks much nicer if every box is a long-winded, woolly paragraph.

To ease the pressure on staff, show goodwill by cancelling one staff meeting nearer the time. They should be able to get a lot done in this time.

Proof reading reports will take a long time, so ask some middle leaders to take on the responsibility. You could even ask them to write some Headteacher comments on the reports too. They will love the opportunity and give them a taste of what it's like to be a Head.

Never accept a teacher's report first time. You must give it back full of corrections and alterations to be made. It's just good leadership. It keeps staff on their toes.

You will always have one teacher who will try to hand in the perfect batch of reports. Sabotage their reports a little if you need to, so you can hand it back for editing. For example, remove a few full stops, or change a 'he' to a 'she' randomly throughout. It's a power thing.

A close colleague of mine alters the report format every year to ensure report writing workload is kept to a maximum. Try to hand out the new format as late as possible to add extra anxiety for staff.

Some schools have introduced termly written reports. I like this a lot. To ease the pressure on staff, reduce the length of the report by two hundred words. This is a decision you can make with your management team. Parents love it and it helps to raise the reputation of the school. Staff hate doing them so be careful.

Consider increasing the number of learning walks and book scrutinies during report writing periods. You will discover a lot about the commitment from your staff as they struggle to balance their workload.

You will discover who has what it takes and who needs to be on a support plan. Under no circumstances should the standard of teaching and learning suffer during report writing periods. It is what it is. Police it very carefully so pupils don't suffer as a result.

Workload

This is an easy one. Whenever you are challenged about excessive workload, you must use the following phrases:

1. It is what it is at the moment.

2. Once Ofsted has been, we can do what we want for a while.

3. We're on a journey.

4. Remember, you get all the holidays.

5. Maybe teaching isn't for you.

At the end of the day, your reputation is on the line. Workload is an important part of your success. Offer to buy staff a big trolley on wheels so they can take their work home if it makes it easier. Staff can always resign if they can't cope with the workload.

PPA

You must give staff a list of things that must be completed in PPA time. You must not let staff work at home. Ever. Seriously, do you expect them to get any work done? Schools that allow this to happen are very naive. Always keep staff at school.

Occasionally, drop into PPA sessions to ensure staff are working hard and not chatting about Bake Off or The Apprentice.

Feel free to use PPA time to organise meetings with teachers. Performance management should always be done during PPA time. Staff won't like it so tell them you're trying to save money. Tell them it's the government's fault.

PPA must only be used for planning, preparation and assessment. Do not allow teachers to catch up with other jobs they haven't had time to do. Discipline staff who do this.

Good luck!

There's so much more I could share with you, but I don't want you to feel too overwhelmed. Start with the tips I have given you so far. It's enough to keep you busy for a while.

Fake Headteacher

About Fake Headteacher

I enjoyed teaching in a few schools early in my career. I was very happy and loved my job immensely.

Then, almost without warning, this was turned upside down when a new management team took over a school I was working at. Within weeks, book scrutinies were being carried out fortnightly, long lists of non-negotiables were introduced, display boards had to look a particular way, slides had to look the same throughout school, teachers' pay was being frozen and support plans were dished out like biscuits in a staff meeting.

Very good teachers resigned - some due to ill health and some found other jobs outside of teaching. Personally, I had a few weeks off as I struggled to come to terms with what was happening.

My mental health suffered, and I found it hard to sleep.

It was one big game that was suddenly being played out in order for the management team to prove their impact on the school. Lessons were deemed inadequate. Teachers were told they weren't good enough. This was a complete shock for many, who had always been told their teaching was good or better in several other schools, including during many Ofsted observations.

It was devastating and I nearly didn't recover. I left the school within a term. I was lucky. I somehow found the mental strength to leave and find another school that I was happy at. However, I soon noticed similar things were being introduced and I didn't like it.

I was beginning to feel like a robot. I had my orders and I had to make sure I followed them. Any autonomy over how I taught was being squeezed out of me. The job was becoming too hard and at the same time, accountability and pressures were increasing. I was working sixty hours a week.

So, I started to write about it. I set up a blog and a twitter page. It helped me share some of the silly things I had seen.

I was surprised when a few people started liking my blogs and commenting on my tweets. It was a great way to let off a bit of steam anonymously.

What happened next was extraordinary. Teachers were contacting me saying their school was managed in the same manner and they wanted to leave the profession. I very quickly realised it wasn't just me. It was happening in a lot of schools.

In a strange way, I was comforted by this. It wasn't me. It was the system. Other teachers started contacting me saying the same thing. 'I love your account because it makes me feel it's not me and I am not alone.'

I also realised that many of my teacher friends were leaving the profession. Lots of them. So many excellent teachers. I felt so sad that the profession had lost these amazing people. It inspired me to write more blogs and continue tweeting.

Now, I write not for my own mental health, but to highlight some of the issues that still exist in some schools.

Some people have accused me of being too negative. Maybe. But it's a reality for so many teachers. So many people don't appreciate what it's like in some schools.

One of the biggest surprises since starting Fake Headteacher was discovering there are some schools out there that are trying to reclaim sensible policies again. This is very reassuring for the future. Hopefully!

I don't know how much longer I will continue to write under the pseudonym of Fake Headteacher. Every month, I think about stopping because I don't need it as a support tool like I used to. Then I see a ridiculous workload tweet or read a direct message from a stressed teacher complaining of silly policies at their school. Then I change my mind.

Thank you to everyone who has enjoyed Fake Headteacher. You have truly helped me get through some very tough times in teaching. I am in a far better place now.

Take care of yourself.

Printed in Great Britain
by Amazon

76849542R00098